HISTORY'S MYSTERIES

The Lost Roanoke Colony

by Megan Cooley Peterson

CAPSTONE PRESS
a capstone imprint

Published by Capstone Press, an imprint of Capstone
1710 Roe Crest Drive, North Mankato, Minnesota 56003
capstonepub.com

Library of Congress Cataloging-in-Publication Data
Names: Peterson, Megan Cooley, author. | Peterson, Megan Cooley. History's mysteries. Title: The lost Roanoke Colony / by Megan Cooley Peterson.
Description: North Mankato, Minnesota : Capstone Press, an imprint of Capstone, [2022] | Series: History's mysteries | Includes bibliographical references and index. | Audience: Ages 8-11 | Audience: Grades 4-6 | Summary: "In 1587, a group of about 115 English settlers arrived on Roanoke Island near North Carolina. They were there to establish an English colony. Later that year, the colony's leader left the island to get supplies. His return trip was delayed. When he finally returned in 1590, the colony and its settlers were gone. What happened to the settlers? Explore the theories behind their disappearance and why it has become one of history's greatest mysteries"-- Provided by publisher.
Identifiers: LCCN 2021028475 (print) | LCCN 2021028476 (ebook) | ISBN 9781663958778 (hardcover) | ISBN 9781666320787 (paperback) | ISBN 9781666320794 (pdf) | ISBN 9781666320817 (Kindle edition)
Subjects: LCSH: Roanoke Colony--History--Juvenile literature. | Roanoke Island (N.C.)--History--Juvenile literature.
Classification: LCC F229 .P48 2022 (print) | LCC F229 (ebook) | DDC 975.6/175--dc23
LC record available at https://lccn.loc.gov/2021028475
LC ebook record available at https://lccn.loc.gov/2021028476

Editorial Credits
Editor: Carrie Sheely; Designer: Kim Pfeffer; Media Researcher: Morgan Walters; Production Specialist: Laura Manthe

Image Credits
Alamy: agefotostock, 21, Ivy Close Images, 8, North Wind Picture Archives, Cover, 5, 7, 13, 25; Associated Press: ASSOCIATED PRESS, 26; Getty Images: Christine_Kohler, 23, Ed Sanford, 24, Heritage Images, 27, Joe Sohm/Visions of America, 28, VW Pics, 17; Newscom: World History Archive, 11; Shutterstock: Jim Lambert, 6, Malachi Jacobs, 15, MarkVanDykePhotography, 18, PRILL, 19, Ryan McGurl, 9

Table of Contents

INTRODUCTION
A Mysterious Disappearance   4

CHAPTER 1
A New Colony   6

CHAPTER 2
Settled on Croatoan Island   14

CHAPTER 3
Moved to the Mainland   20

CHAPTER 4
Death by Disease or Attacks   24

CHAPTER 5
The Mystery Remains   28

Cold Case File   29
Glossary   30
Read More   31
Internet Sites   31
Index   32

Words in **bold** are in the glossary.

A Mysterious Disappearance

On August 15, 1590, two British ships sailed near Roanoke Island in North America. The *Moonlight* and *Hopewell* had carried food, clothing, and other supplies across the Atlantic. Governor John White stood on the deck of the *Hopewell*, scanning the coastline. It had been three years since he left behind more than 100 **colonists**. He was eager to see them again.

Soon White found the **colony** he had helped build three years ago. But no one was there, and there was no sign of a struggle. All the houses they had built had been taken down. Carved into one of the wooden posts surrounding the settlement was a single word—*CROATOAN*. The colonists had vanished. But where had they gone?

When John White returned to Roanoke Island in 1590, he found the colony he had helped form mysteriously abandoned.

CHAPTER 1

A New Colony

On May 8, 1587, about 115 men, women, and children set sail from England. They were going to start a new British colony on the east coast of North America. They had no idea that their adventure would become a great mystery. More than 400 years later, people are still trying to find out what happened to them.

Traveling by ship in the 1500s was not easy. The colonists ate mostly cheese and dried biscuits called **hardtack** on the journey. They slept on the floor. Many likely suffered from seasickness.

Hardtack is very dry with little flavor.

COMPETING COUNTRIES

By the late 1500s, Spain had established several colonies in the Caribbean and North America. England, afraid of falling behind, wanted to set up a colony of its own. A colony in North America also made it easier for them to raid Spanish ships crossing the Atlantic. These ships carried gold, silver, sugar, silks, and other goods. At the time, the governments of some countries hired pirates to steal for them.

Colonists who crossed the Atlantic Ocean to colonize North America could have spent more than two months at sea.

A New Beginning

The colonists' journey to North America took two months. On July 22, 1587, the ships anchored at Port Ferdinando on Croatoan Island, now called Hatteras Island. White's daughter, Eleanor Dare, and her husband, Ananias, were among the colonists. White led them to a former settlement on Roanoke Island. Together, they repaired existing homes and built new ones. They did their best to make a new life in an unfamiliar place.

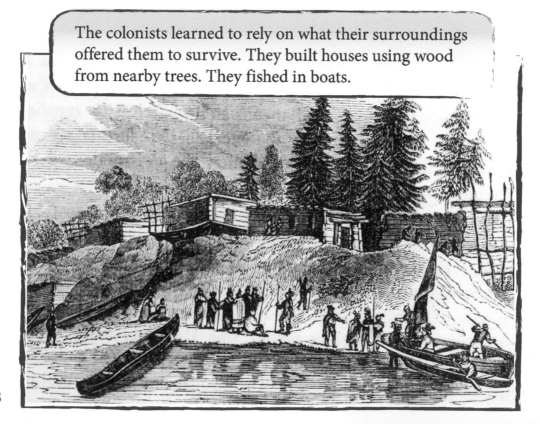

The colonists learned to rely on what their surroundings offered them to survive. They built houses using wood from nearby trees. They fished in boats.

The First Roanoke Colony

Governor John White had been to Roanoke Island once before. He traveled there in 1585 with a group of English soldiers to set up a colony. White, an artist, was given the job of painting local plants and Native American life.

The area around Roanoke, called the Outer Banks, has shallow water in many places. Most of the men's food was destroyed when their ship ran aground. They relied on Native Americans for survival.

Fact

The Outer Banks are nicknamed "The Graveyard of the Atlantic." As many as 3,000 ships may have wrecked there.

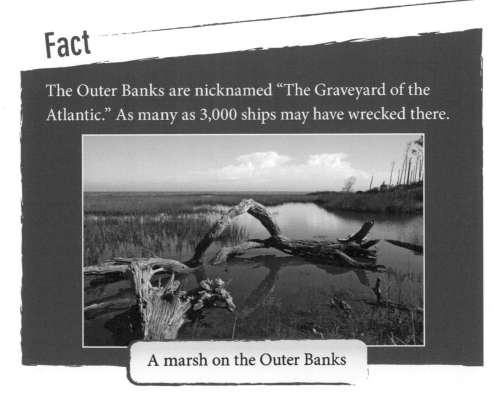

A marsh on the Outer Banks

Chief Wingina, leader of Native American tribes in the area, welcomed the men. He let them set up camp on the island and gave them food. But the colonists soon grew distrustful and violent toward the Native Americans. They even killed Wingina. After almost starving to death, the men returned to England in 1586.

Trouble

White's second attempt to settle on Roanoke got off to a bad start. Only a few days after landing, a colonist went swimming alone. He was shot with 16 arrows and died. Native Americans had possibly wanted to get **revenge** for Chief Wingina's murder. At the end of August, the colonists felt they would have a better chance at survival with more supplies and people. They convinced White to sail back to England.

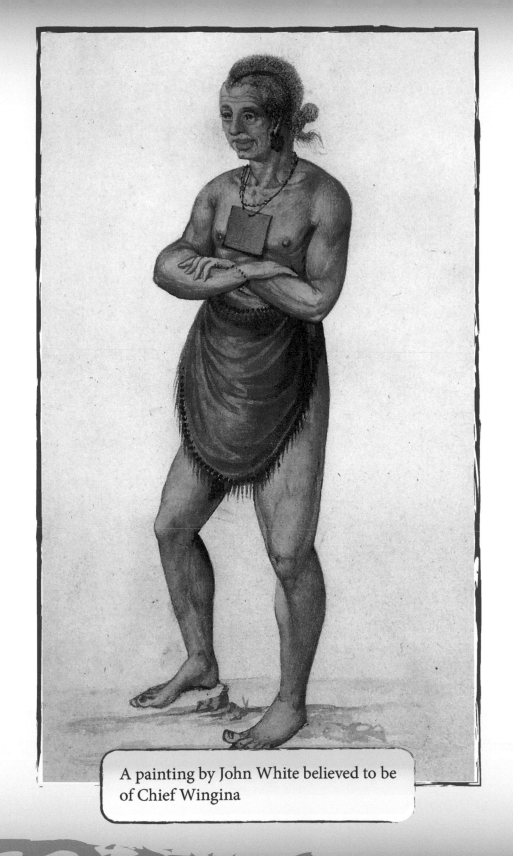

A painting by John White believed to be of Chief Wingina

White's decision to leave would be a costly one. He didn't know that war was breaking out between England and Spain. Because of this, White couldn't get back to North America right away. When he finally returned to Roanoke in 1590, White believed the colonists had moved to Croatoan Island. But he and his men never made it there to search. The wind blew them off course, and they were forced to go back to England. White never returned to Roanoke. He died in 1593.

Fact

In August 1587, Eleanor Dare gave birth to a girl named Virginia. She was the first English child born in North America.

Eleanor and her husband, Ananias Dare, had Virginia baptized soon after her birth.

Settled on Croatoan Island

More than 400 years have passed since the Roanoke colonists settled off North Carolina's coast. Interest in what happened to them has only grown with time. After John White failed to find the colonists, he wrote a report. In his writings, White said he and the colonists had discussed leaving Roanoke. They planned to move either to Croatoan Island or west onto the mainland. Croatoan Island was 50 miles (80 kilometers) south of Roanoke.

The colonists also came up with a code. If the colonists left Roanoke, they would carve their new location. If they left in a panic, they would also add a cross. No cross was carved along with *CROATOAN*. White believed that meant they left peacefully. He felt certain they were safe on Croatoan Island or the mainland.

Croatoan Island, now known as Hatteras Island, is 50 miles (80 km) long.

Life on Croatoan

What could have happened to the colonists after they moved to Croatoan? They may have lived with the Croatoan Indians or other Native Americans. They would have **adapted** to their **cultures**. As their woolen clothing wore out, the colonists may have worn deerskin. They would have learned to speak Algonquian. They may have learned to hunt with bows and arrows instead of guns.

Long-Lost Relatives?

In the late 1800s, the Lumbee Indians provided a clue. While asking the U.S. government for aid, they said they were **descendants** of the lost colony members. Some **ancestors** of the Lumbee came from Croatoan Island. Many Lumbee have fair skin and light-colored eyes.

In the early 2000s, researchers tested this claim using **DNA**. A few Lumbee members agreed to be tested. Many tests showed a high amount of European ancestry. But no one has found any bones of the Roanoke colonists or their relatives. Until then, scientists can't trace the DNA back to the lost colonists.

Some Lumbee Indians have green eyes, which shows they have European ancestry.

Fact

The Lumbee Tribe was officially recognized by North Carolina in 1885. At that time, they were called the Croatan Indians.

Digging for Clues

Croatoan Island holds clues of its own. A village once stood near Cape Creek on the island. Many historians have focused on this spot. They have dug there hoping to uncover items the lost colonists used.

People digging there found a brass engraved ring in 1998. The ring had a lion engraved on it. It was made in the 1500s in England. Could it have belonged to a lost colonist? Researchers found the ring mixed with objects from the 1600s. These were made after the colonists arrived. Researchers aren't sure if the ring belonged to a Roanoke colonist. It may have belonged to a colonist who came to North America in the 1600s.

Hatteras Island isn't well populated year-round, which has helped make digging for artifacts there easier.

Researchers have found other European objects at Cape Creek. They dug up the metal handle of a light sword. This type of sword was used in England in the 1500s. They also found a **slate** writing tablet that English people used in the 1500s.

Sword handles from long ago are often very decorative. Their design helps historians know how old they are and where they are from.

CHAPTER 3

Moved to the Mainland

When John White failed to return to Roanoke, the colonists had a choice to make. They could stay on the island or move somewhere else. In his report, White said he and the colonists discussed moving 50 miles (80 km) west onto the mainland. It's possible the colonists went there.

Mystery of the Map

While in Roanoke, White drew many maps of the Outer Banks. One survives to this day in the British Museum. In 2012, a researcher studying the map noticed it had a patch. The patch covered a spot on the mainland where the Chowan and Roanoke Rivers meet.

Researchers found a hidden symbol under the patch. The symbol showed the location of a fort. Perhaps that's where the colonists went or planned to build a fort. But at that time, mapmakers placed patches on mistakes and then painted over them. It's possible White had simply made a mistake.

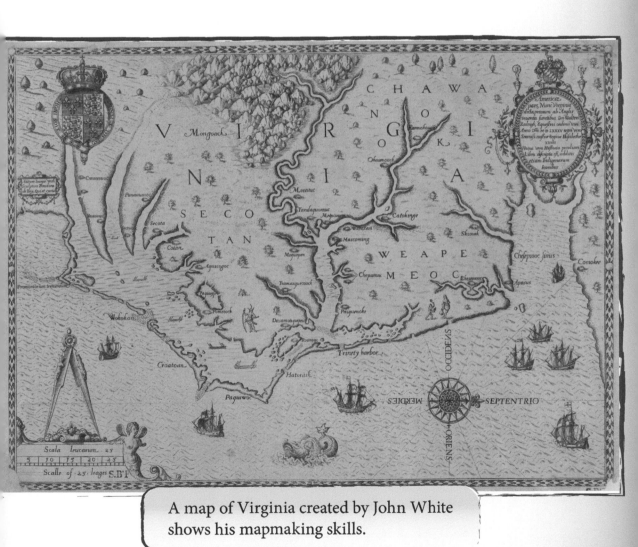

A map of Virginia created by John White shows his mapmaking skills.

Sites X and Y

Researchers decided to investigate the hidden fort symbol. They began digging in that area, which they called Site X. They uncovered European pottery pieces that dated back to the 1500s. But they did not find any evidence that a fort or structure had been built on Site X.

In 2019, researchers moved to a site nearby named Site Y. There, they found even more pottery pieces from the 1500s. They found pieces of English dishes used to store and eat food. Does this prove the Roanoke colonists lived at these places? Historians are still unsure.

THE JAMESTOWN CONNECTION

In 1607, England set up its first permanent colony in North America. Jamestown was about 150 miles (241 km) north of Roanoke in present-day Virginia. John Smith, a Jamestown colonist, met with Chief Powhatan, leader of the Powhatan Indians. Powhatan reportedly told Smith that English people were living south of Roanoke on the mainland. But after searching, no one ever found any signs of the colonists.

John Smith and other colonists met the Chesapeake Indians after arriving in Chesapeake Bay.

CHAPTER 4

Death by Disease or Attacks

On November 8, 1937, a man named Louis Hammond walked into Emory University in Atlanta, Georgia. Hammond had found a large stone near the Chowan River in North Carolina. He asked to speak to someone about some markings on the stone.

The Chowan River flows near the border between North Carolina and Virginia.

Emory professors examined the 21-pound (9.5-kilogram) stone. They found words etched into it. Two names stuck out to them: Ananias and Virginia Dare. The writing said they died in 1591. It was signed *EWD*. Did the letters stand for Eleanor White Dare?

The other side of the stone said the lost colonists had moved to the Chowan River area. For two years, it read, they suffered "only misery and war." Disease killed many of them. Native Americans killed others, including Eleanor's husband and daughter. The stone said they were buried 4 miles (6 km) east of the river. Another stone was said to mark their grave.

A horseback rider gallops through the Roanoke colony to warn colonists of a possible upcoming attack by Native Americans.

A Hoax?

In 1939, stonecutter Bill Eberhardt found a second stone. It listed the names of 17 dead colonists. In total, Eberhardt brought 42 stones to the Emory professors. But the lettering style on Eberhardt's stones looked nothing like the lettering on the first stone. He later admitted the stones were faked. Does this mean the original stone was also a **hoax**? Today, researchers still can't agree if the first stone is real or fake.

Dr. H. J. Pearce and his son H. J. Pearce Jr. studied stones found near Greenville, South Carolina, that reportedly tell of the burial of some of the Roanoke colonists.

Killed by the Spanish

In spring 1587, Spain's King Philip II received a troubling report. His spies said the English were trying to form a colony in the New World to raid Spanish ships. Philip sent men to find the English colonists and stop them. Some historians say the Spanish may have captured or killed the colonists at Roanoke. But Spanish records from that time make no mention of an attack on Roanoke.

King Philip II of Spain

CHAPTER 5

The Mystery Remains

More than 400 years have passed since the Roanoke colonists vanished from history. No one can say for certain what happened all those years ago in the North Carolina wilderness. Did they settle somewhere else? Did they die from disease or in an attack? One of America's oldest mysteries has yet to be solved.

A gravestone in remembrance of the Lost Colony of Roanoke at Roanoke, North Carolina

The Main Theories

1. Moved to Croatoan Island

When John White returned to Roanoke in 1590, he found *CROATOAN* carved into a post. White believed the colonists probably went to the island. Many historians agree that at least some of the colonists went there.

2. Moved to the Mainland

In White's report, he said the colonists may have also gone to the Chowan River area. A fort symbol on a map he drew may have marked a possible settlement site. English pottery found there supports the idea that some of the colonists moved to the mainland. This is another widely accepted theory among historians.

3. Killed by Attacks

It's possible the rest of the colonists were killed by Native Americans. But White saw no signs of violence. Spain's King Philip also ordered his men to find the Roanoke colony and drive them away. But there's no record they ever found it.

4. Death from Disease

Writing on the Dare Stone said that some of the colonists died from disease. Eleanor Dare allegedly created the stone. But no one knows for certain if the stone is real or fake.

Glossary

adapt (uh-DAPT)—to change to fit into a new or different environment

ancestor (AN-ses-tuhr)—a member of a person's family who lived a long time ago

colonist (KAH-luh-nist)—a person who settles in a new territory that is governed by his or her home country

colony (KAH-luh-nee)—an area that has been settled by people from another country; a colony is ruled by another country

culture (KUHL-chuhr)—a people's way of life, ideas, art, customs, and traditions

descendant (di-SEN-duhnt)—someone who can trace their family roots back to one person or a group of people

DNA—material in cells that gives people their individual characteristics; DNA stands for deoxyribonucleic acid

hardtack (HARD-tak)—a hard, saltless biscuit once used as food rations for armies and on board ships

hoax (HOHKS)—a trick to make people believe something that is not true

revenge (ree-VENJ)—striking back after a wrongdoing

slate (SLAYT)—fine-grained metamorphic rock that splits into thin, smooth-surfaced layers

Read More

Jazynka, Kitson. *History's Mysteries: Curious Clues, Cold Cases, and Puzzles from the Past.* Washington, D.C.: National Geographic Kids, 2017.

Schuetz, Kari. *Roanoke: The Lost Colony.* Minneapolis: Bellwether Media, Inc., 2018.

Schweizer, Chris. *The Roanoke Colony: America's First Mystery.* New York: First Second, 2020.

Internet Sites

Britannica Kids: Lost Colony
kids.britannica.com/students/article/Lost-Colony/315475

Ducksters: Lost Colony of Roanoke
ducksters.com/history/colonial_america/lost_colony_of_roanoke.php

National Park Service: Roanoke Island in the 1500s
nps.gov/fora/learn/historyculture/roanoke-island-in-the-1500s.htm

Wonderopolis: What Happened to the Lost Colony?
wonderopolis.org/wonder/what-happened-to-the-lost-colony

Index

Croatoan Island, 8, 12, 14, 15, 16, 18, 29

Dare, Ananias, 8, 13, 25
Dare, Eleanor, 8, 12, 13, 25, 29
Dare, Virginia, 12, 13, 25

England, 6, 7, 10, 12, 18, 19, 23

Hatteras Island. *See* Croatoan Island

Jamestown, 23

King Philip II, 27, 29

mainland, 14, 20, 23, 29
maps, 20, 21, 29

Native Americans, 9, 10, 15, 25, 29
    Chesapeake Indians, 23

Chief Powhatan, 23
Chief Wingina, 10, 11
Croatoan Indians, 15
Lumbee Indians, 16, 17
Powhatan Indians, 23
North America, 4, 6, 7, 8, 12, 18, 23

Outer Banks, 9, 20

pottery, 22, 29

rings, 18

Smith, John, 23
Spain, 7, 12, 27, 29
stones, 24, 25, 26, 29
swords, 19

White, John, 4, 5, 8, 9, 10, 11, 12, 14, 20, 21, 29

Author Biography

Megan Cooley Peterson is a writer, editor, and bookworm. When she isn't writing or reading, you can find her watching movies or planning her next Halloween party. She lives in Minnesota with her husband and daughter.